FM 30-35

BASIC FIELD MANUAL

✻

MILITARY INTELLİGENCE
IDENTIFICATION OF GERMAN AIRCRAFT

Prepared under direction of the
Chief of Staff

UNITED STATES
GOVERNMENT PRINTING OFFICE
WASHINGTON : 1942

WAR DEPARTMENT,
WASHINGTON, March 11, 1942.
FM 30–35, Military Intelligence, Identification of German Aircraft, is published for the information and guidance of all concerned.

[A. G. 062.11 (1–14–42).]

BY ORDER OF THE SECRETARY OF WAR:

G. C. MARSHALL,
Chief of Staff.

OFFICIAL:

J. A. ULIO,
Major General,
The Adjutant General.

LIST OF ILLUSTRATIONS

LIST OF ILLUSTRATIONS

BASIC FIELD MANUAL

MILITARY INTELLIGENCE

IDENTIFICATION OF GERMAN AIRCRAFT

(This manual supersedes FM 30–35, July 5, 1941.)

The material contained in this manual has been secured from many sources. It is the best material available but may be incomplete and, in some respects, inaccurate.

This manual containing illustrations with explanatory data relative to German aircraft is published for distribution. It will be used for instruction of officers and men in appearance and general characteristics of German aircraft.

The German airplane markings are as shown below:

GERMANY

WING   TAIL

NOTE.—Shaded area of tail-marking indicates red background.

**MILITARY
AIRCRAFT**

GERMAN
ARMY

FIGHTER ARADO AR–197

Description:	Round tip, straight-wing, staggered biplane of unequal span, slightly dihedral, inclosed cockpit, single-engine, blunt nose, fixed landing gear.
Crew:	One.
Armament:	Machine guns and bomb.
Ammunition:	
Bomb load:	
Radio:	
Armor:	
Motors:	One nine-cylinder BMW radial.
Maximum speed:	
Rate of climb:	
Service ceiling:	
Maximum range:	
Wing span:	

4

Fighter
ARADO AR–197

GERMAN
ARMY

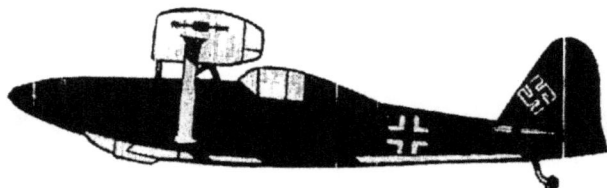

FIGHTER FOCKE-WULF FW-159

Description: High-wing, parasol type monoplane, in-
                   closed cockpit, single-engine, long ta-
                   pered nose, retractable landing gear.
Crew: One.
Armament: Two fixed machine guns.
Ammunition:
Bomb load:
Radio:
Armor:
Motors: One 1,000-horsepower Daimler Benz DB
                   600G.
Maximum speed:
Rate of climb:
Service ceiling:
Maximum range:
Wing span:

IDENTIFICATION OF GERMAN AIRCRAFT

Fighter
FOCKE-WULF FW–159

GERMAN
ARMY

FIGHTER FOCKE-WULF FW–190

Description:	Single-engine, low-wing monoplane; side view resembles P–36, front view, an Arado Ar–96, and wing form, a Spitfire; fairly short fuselage.
Crew:	One.
Armament:	Four machine guns, three cannon.
Ammunition:	
Bomb load:	
Radio:	
Armor:	
Motors:	One 1,500-horsepower BMW 802.
Maximum speed:	380 miles per hour.
Rate of climb:	
Service ceiling:	38,000 feet.
Maximum range:	380 miles.
Wing span:	30 feet.

Fighter
FOCKE-WULF FW–190

GERMAN
ARMY

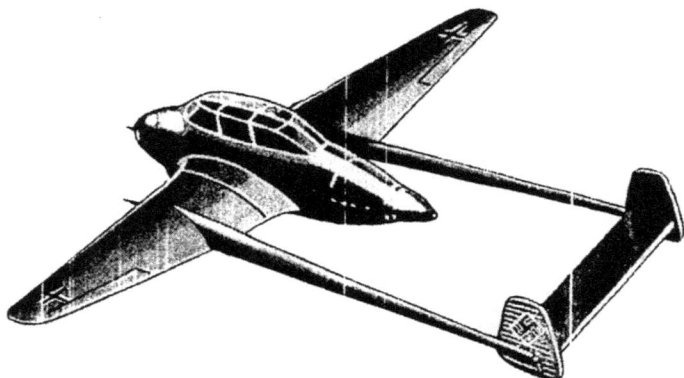

PURSUIT FOCKE-WULF FW-198

Description:	Tapered, mid-wing monoplane, all metal, single pusher type motor, short, blunt nose, inclosed cockpit, twin tail boom and rudder fins.
Crew:	One.
Armament:	Two cannon in boom extension forward; four machine guns in nose.
Ammunition:	
Bomb load:	
Radio:	Two-way.
Armor:	
Motors:	One 1,360-horsepower DB 601E.
Maximum speed:	370 miles per hour at 19,000 feet
Rate of climb:	2,750 feet per minute.
Service ceiling:	34,500.
Maximum range:	590 miles.
Wing span:	

10

Pursuit
FOCKE-WULF FW–198

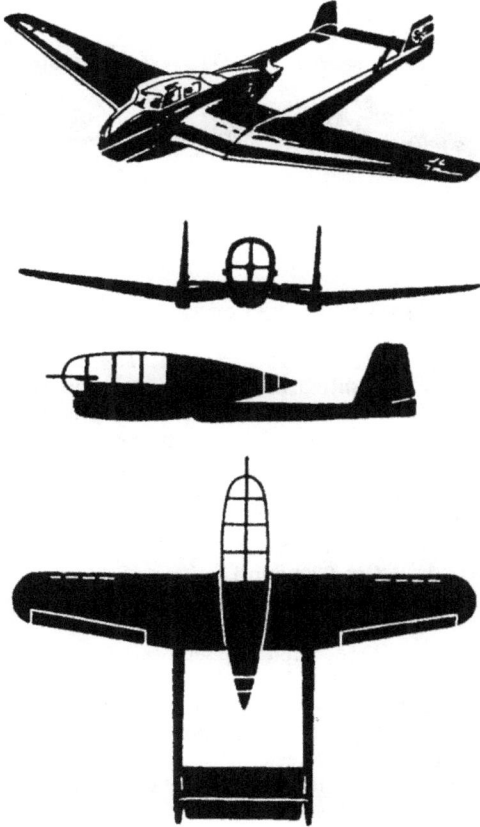

GERMAN
ARMY

FIGHTER HEINKEL HE–112

Description:	Round tip, tapered, slightly swept-back, dihedral, low-wing monoplane, inclosed cockpit, single-engine, long pointed nose, retractable landing gear.
Crew:	One.
Armament:	Two cannon and two machine guns.
Ammunition:	600 rounds per machine gun; 100 rounds per cannon.
Bomb load:	Six 22-pound.
Radio:	
Armor:	
Motors:	One 1,150 horsepower Daimler Benz DB 601A.
Maximum speed:	354 miles per hour.
Rate of climb:	2,760 feet per minute.
Service ceiling:	31,700 feet.
Maximum range:	715 miles at 282 miles per hour.
Wing span:	30 feet.

Fighter
HEINKEL HE–112

GERMAN
ARMY

PURSUIT HEINKEL HE-113

Description:	Long, tapered, trapezoidal, slightly dihedral low-wing, all metal monoplane, pointed nose, single-motor, inclosed cockpit, inward retractable landing gear, and retractable tail wheel.
Crew:	One.
Armament:	Two large-caliber machine guns situated in wings near fuselage and three cannon.
Ammunition:	
Bomb load:	
Radio:	Two-way.
Armor:	Similar to ME-109, rear and above only.
Motors:	One 1,500-horsepower Daimler Benz, DB 603.
Maximum speed:	400 miles per hour at 19,000 feet.
Rate of climb:	3,000 feet per minute.
Service ceiling:	37,000 feet.
Maximum range:	650 miles.
Wing span:	31 feet.

Pursuit
HEINKEL HE–113

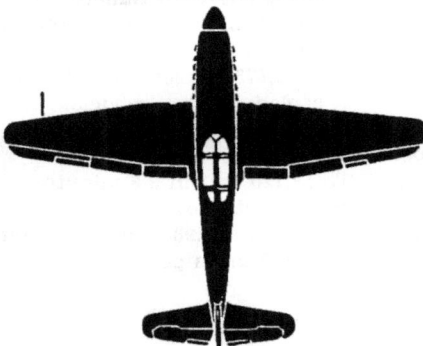

GERMAN
· ARMY

PURSUIT MESSERSCHMITT ME–109E

Description:	Tapered, square tip, low-wing monoplane, all metal, single-motor, pointed nose, inclosed cockpit, and retractable landing gear.
Crew:	One.
Armament:	Two machine guns, fixed-fuselage, and two 20-mm cannon, fixed-wing (or four machine guns). (Latest model cannon through propeller.)
Ammunition:	500 rounds per machine gun; 60 rounds per 20-mm.
Bomb load:	Can carry one 500-pound bomb.
Radio:	Two-way.
Armor:	8-mm armor protection for pilot from rear and above. Bulletproof windshield. Fuel tanks partially protected but not self-sealing.
Motors:	One 1,175-horsepower, DB 601A, liquid-cooled. (New models: 1,500 to 1,700 horsepower, DB 603.)
Maximum speed:	354 miles per hour.
Rate of climb:	To 13,120 feet in 3.8 minutes.
Service ceiling:	36,080 feet.
Maximum range:	620 miles at 298 miles per hour; 540 miles at 322 miles per hour.
Wing span:	33 feet.

Pursuit
MESSERSCHMITT ME–109E

GERMAN
ARMY

FIGHTER MESSERSCHMITT ME-109 F1

Description:	Round tip, tapered, slightly swept-back, dihedral, low-wing monoplane, inclosed cockpit, single-engine, long pointed nose, retractable landing gear.
Crew:	One.
Armament:	Two cannon and two machine guns.
Ammunition:	
Bomb load:	550 pounds.
Radio:	Two-way.
Armor:	8-mm. armor in roofpiece and rear; bullet-proof windshield.
Motors:	One 1,450-horsepower Daimler Benz DB 601N
Maximum speed:	380 miles per hour.
Rate of climb:	
Service ceiling:	40,000 feet.
Maximum range:	560 miles at 248 miles per hour.
Wing span:	33 feet.

Fighter
MESSERSCHMITT ME–109 F1

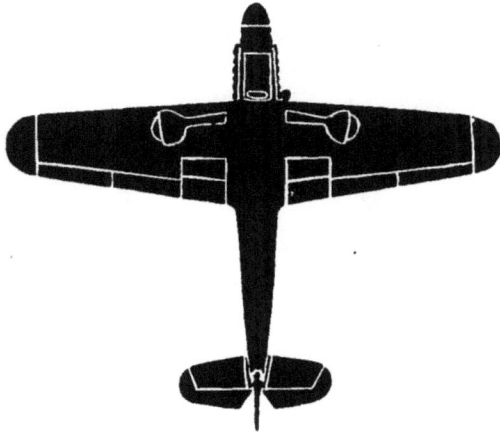

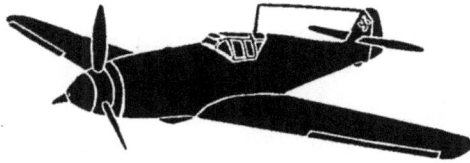

GERMAN
ARMY

FIGHTER MESSERSCHMITT ME–115

Description:
Crew:
Armament: Two cannon and two machine guns.
Ammunition:
Bomb load:
Radio:
Armor:
Motors: One 2,000-horsepower Daimler Benz DB 605.
Maximum speed: 400 miles per hour.
Rate of climb:
Service ceiling:
Maximum range:
Wing span:

Fighter
MESSERSCHMITT ME–115

GERMAN
ARMY

PURSUIT FOCKE-WULF FW-187

Description:	Low-wing cantilever monoplane, thin wing, twin motors projecting noticeably from wings, pointed nose, retractable landing gear.
Crew:	Two.
Armament:	Four machine guns; two 20-mm cannon.
Ammunition:	
Bomb load:	Light bombs carried externally.
Radio:	Two-way.
Armor:	
Motors:	Two 1,400-horsepower, DB 603.
Maximum speed:	395 miles per hour.
Rate of climb:	To 6,560 feet in 1.9 minutes.
Service ceiling:	38,700 feet.
Maximum range:	650 miles.
Wing span:	51 feet.

Pursuit
FOCKE-WULF FW–187

GERMAN
ARMY

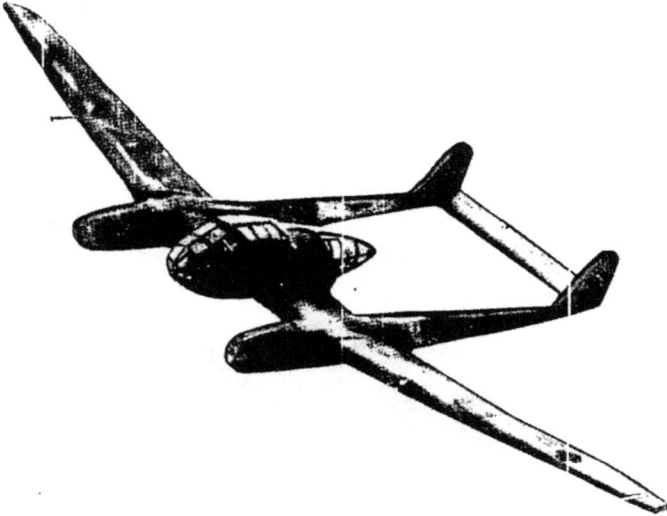

FIGHTER FOCKE-WULF FW-189

Description: Round tip, decidedly swept-back, dihedral,
                  low-wing monoplane, inclosed cockpit,
                  twin engines, twin tail boom and rudders,
                  retractable landing gear.
Crew: Three.
Armament: Four machine guns.
Ammunition:
Bomb load:
Radio:
Armor:
Motors: Two 450-horsepower Argus 32 410 A1.
Maximum speed: 222 miles per hour.
Rate of climb: 1,640 feet in 1 minute.
Service ceiling: 27,500 feet.
Maximum range:
Wing span: 60 feet.

24

Fighter
FOCKE-WULF FW–189

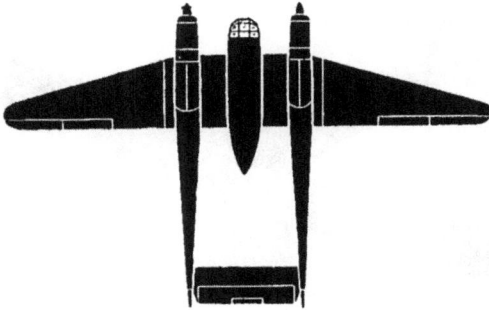

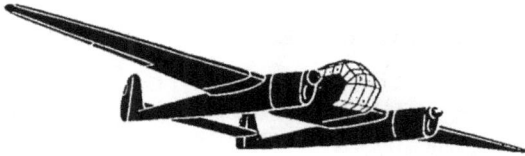

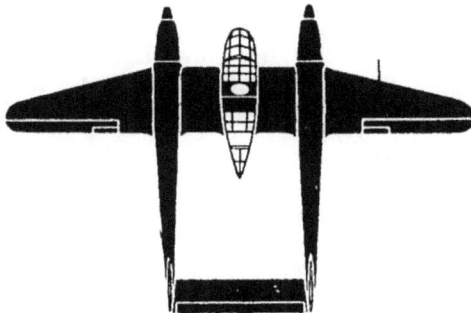

GERMAN
ARMY

PURSUIT MESSERSCHMITT ME–110

Description:	Long, narrow, slightly swept-back and tapered, low-wing monoplane, two mid-wing motors, pointed engine nacelles, inclosed cockpit, retractable landing gear, and twin rudder fins.
Crew:	Three.
Armament:	Four machine guns, fixed-fuselage; two machine guns, flexible-fuselage, rear; two 20-mm cannon, fixed-nose.
Ammunition:	5,000 rounds machine gun; 400 rounds 20-mm.
Bomb load:	Can carry one 1,100-pound bomb.
Radio:	Two-way and blind landing equipment.
Armor:	9-mm in front; bulletproof windshield.
Motors:	Two 1,175-horsepower DB 601A, liquid-cooled.
Maximum speed:	370 miles per hour.
Rate of climb:	10,000 feet in 4.1 minutes; 20,000 feet in 10.1 minutes.
Service ceiling:	30,000 feet.
Maximum range:	1,800 miles.
Wing span:	55 feet.

Pursuit
MESSERSCHMITT ME–110

27

GERMAN
ARMY

DIVE BOMBER BLOHM AND VOSS-137A

Description:	Round tip, tapered, swept-back, negative dihedral, low-wing monoplane, open cockpit, single-engine, blunt nose, fixed landing gear.
Crew:	One.
Armament:	Four fixed machine guns.
Ammunition:	
Bomb load:	One 550-pound bomb.
Radio:	
Armor:	
Motors:	One 770-horsepower BMW 132A.
Maximum speed:	211 miles per hour.
Rate of climb:	2,100 feet per minute.
Service ceiling:	23,000 feet.
Maximum range:	320 miles.
Wing span:	37 feet.

Dive Bomber
BLOHM AND VOSS–137A

GERMAN
ARMY

DIVE BOMBER HENSCHEL HS–123

Description: Round tip, straight-winged, staggered, cut-
                 out biplane of unequal span open cock-
                 pit, single-engine, fixed landing gear.
Crew:
Armament: Two machine guns.
Ammunition:
Bomb load: 1,100 pounds.
Radio:
Armor:
Motors: One 880-horsepower BMW 132 DC.
Maximum speed: 225 miles per hour.
Rate of climb:
Service ceiling: 27,500 feet.
Maximum range: 650 miles.
Wing span:

Dive Bomber
HENSCHEL HS–123

GERMAN
ARMY

DIVE BOMBER JUNKERS JU–87
("STUKA" DIVE BOMBERS)

Description:	Slightly swept-back, tapered, negative dihedral, square tip, low-wing monoplane, all metal, single-motor, inclosed cockpit, long pointed nose, square-tip tail plane, and fixed landing gear.
Crew:	Two.
Armament:	Two machine guns, fixed-fuselage; one machine gun, flexible-fuselage, rear.
Ammunition:	
Bomb load:	One 1,100-pound and two 55-pound.
Radio:	Two-way.
Armor:	
Motors:	One 1,200-horsepower Junkers Jumo 211A, liquid-cooled.
Maximum speed:	242 to 250 miles per hour. Diving speed, 430 miles per hour.
Rate of climb:	To 13,120 feet in 8.5 minutes.
Service ceiling:	27,890 feet.
Maximum range:	498 miles at 186 miles per hour.
Wing span:	45 feet.

Dive Bomber
JUNKERS JU–87
("STUKA" DIVE BOMBERS)

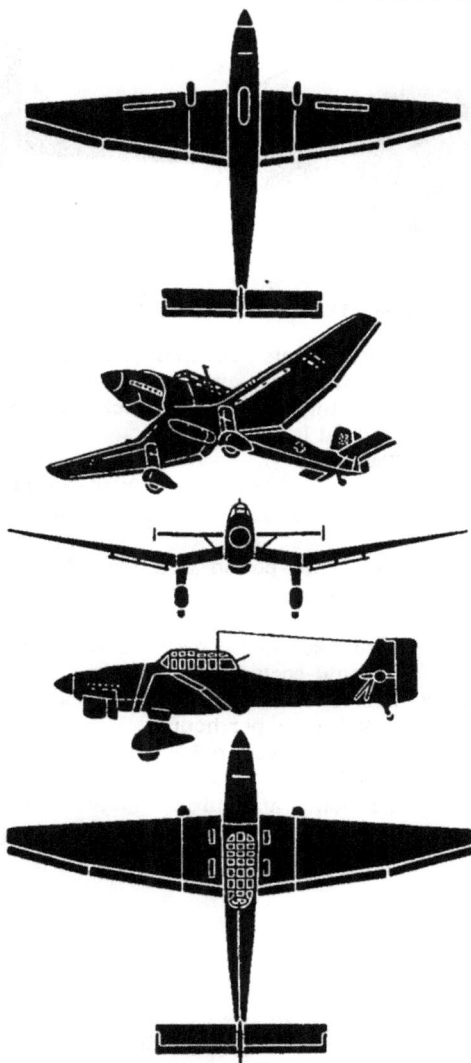

33

GERMAN
ARMY

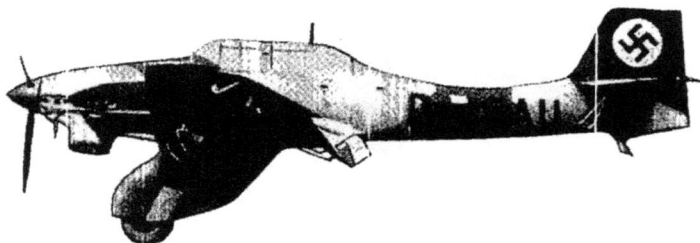

DIVE BOMBER JUNKERS JU–87K

Description: Swept-back, tapered, negative dihedral.
round tip, low-wing monoplane, single-
motor, pointed nose, inclosed cockpit, and
fixed landing gear.

Crew: Two.

Armament: Two machine guns, fixed-fuselage; one
machine gun, flexible-fuselage, rear.

Ammunition:

Bomb load: One 1,100-pound and two 110-pound.

Radio: Two-way.

Armor:

Motors: One 1,200-horsepower Junkers Jumo 211A,
liquid-cooled.

Maximum speed: 242 to 250 miles per hour. Diving speed,
430 miles per hour.

Rate of climb: To 13,120 feet in 8.5 minutes.

Service ceiling: 27,890 feet.

Maximum range: 2.5 hours at cruising speed; 498 miles at
186 miles per hour.

Wing span: 45 feet.

Dive Bomber
JUNKERS JU–87K

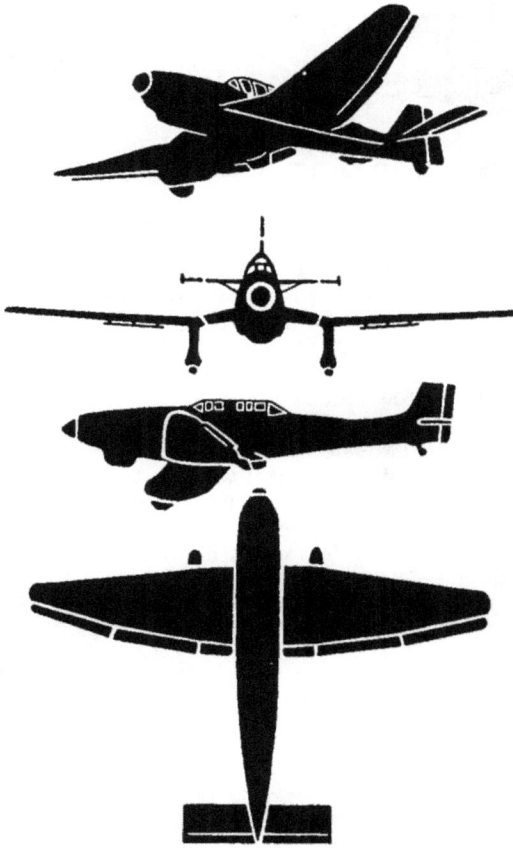

GERMAN
ARMY

DIVE BOMBER OR LIGHT BOMBER JUNKERS JU–88

Description:	Swept-back, tapered, round tip, midwing monoplane, all metal, twin midwing motors, blunt engine nacelles, short round nose, retractable landing gear, and elliptical tail plane.
Crew:	Four (three when used as dive bomber).
Armament:	Five or six machine guns; one cannon.
Ammunition:	500 rounds per gun.
Bomb load:	4,960 pounds.
Radio:	Two-way and interphone.
Armor:	Self-seal tanks; well armored in vital areas.
Motors:	Two 1,200-horsepower Junkers Jumo 211.
Maximum speed:	310 miles per hour.
Rate of climb:	15,000 feet in 7.1 minutes.
Service ceiling:	29,520 feet.
Maximum range:	1,560 miles at 185 miles per hour
Wing span:	60 feet.

Dive Bomber or Light Bomber
JUNKERS JU–88

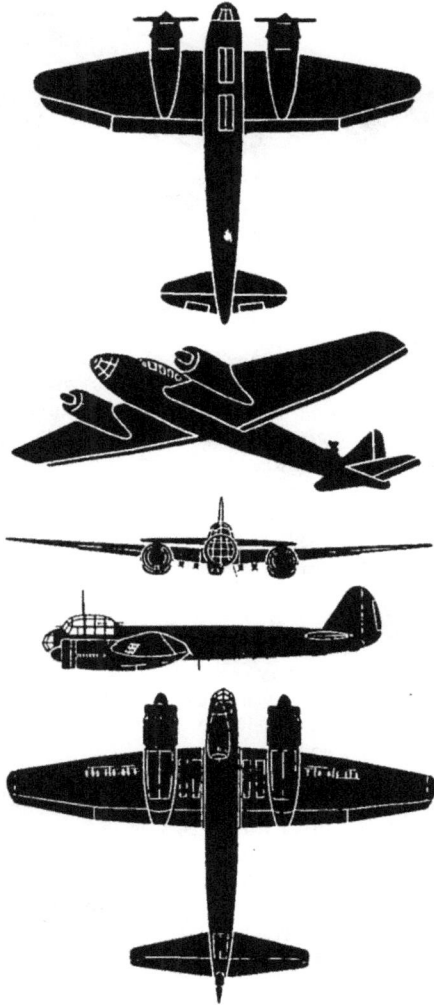

GERMAN
ARMY

LIGHT BOMBER DORNIER DO-17

Description:	Slightly swept-back, tapered, round tip, high-wing monoplane, twin motors, blunt engine nacelles protruding below the wings, long pointed nose, retractable landing gear and tail wheel, and twin rudder fins.
Crew:	Three, all in one compartment.
Armament:	Eight flexible machine guns—upper and lower forward, upper and lower rear, two on each side.
Ammunition:	
Bomb load:	Two 1,100-pound.
Radio:	Two-way.
Armor:	Armor protection for crew.
Motors:	Two 1,050-horsepower DB 600, liquid-cooled.
Maximum speed:	288 miles per hour.
Rate of climb:	To 3,280 feet in 1.8 minutes; to 19,680 feet in 17 minutes.
Service ceiling:	29,283 feet.
Maximum range:	965 to 1,860 miles, depending upon gas and bomb load or 1,200 miles at 210 miles per hour.
Wing span:	59 feet.

Light Bomber
DORNIER DO–17

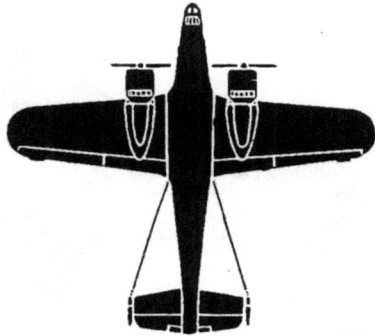

39

GERMAN
ARMY

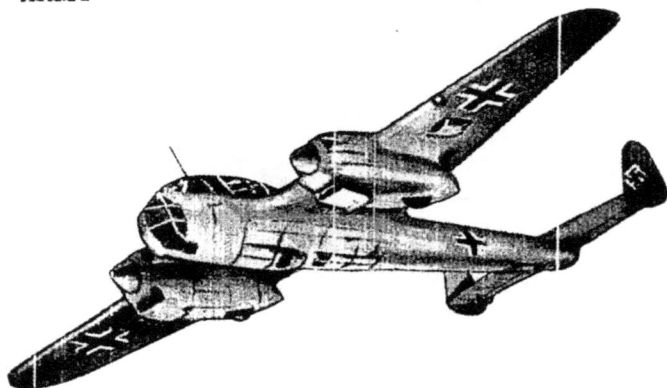

LIGHT BOMBER DORNIER DO-215

Description:	Slightly swept-back, tapered, round tip. high-wing monoplane, all metal, twin motors, pronounced engine nacelles extending below wings, retractable landing gear and tail wheel, and twin rudder fins.
Crew:	Four, all in one compartment.
Armament:	Five machine guns—one front, one each, upper and lower rear, one each. beams.
Ammunition:	
Bomb load:	Two 1,100-pound.
Radio:	Two-way.
Armor:	Fuel tanks and crew protected.
Motors:	Two 1,150-horsepower DB 601, liquid-cooled.
Maximum speed:	312 miles per hour at 16,400 feet.
Rate of climb:	To 3,280 feet in 1.8 minutes; to 16,400 feet in 12.8 minutes.
Service ceiling:	27,230 feet.
Maximum range:	965 to 1,860 miles, depending upon gas and bomb load; 1,044 at 264 miles per hour.
Wing span:	59 feet.

Light Bomber
DORNIER DO-215

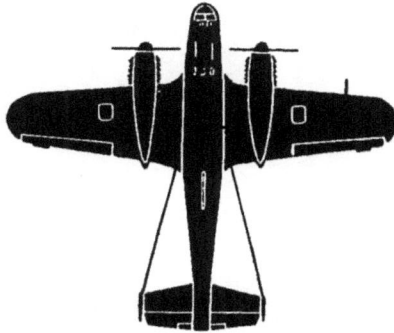

GERMAN
ARMY

LIGHT BOMBER DORNIER DO-217

Description:	High-wing monoplane, similar to enlarged Do-17; twin engines, large transparent bulbous nose; bomb doors form long bulge running almost whole length of fuselage giving profile deep appearance; twin tail fin and rudders.
Crew:	Three or four.
Armament:	Six machine guns and two cannon.
Ammunition:	
Bomb load:	4,000 pounds.
Radio:	
Armor:	Extensive and complete.
Motors:	Two 1,600-horsepower Junkers Jumo 801.
Maximum speed:	340 miles per hour.
Rate of climb:	
Service ceiling:	
Maximum range:	1,800 miles with 4,000 pounds.
Wing span:	65 to 70 feet.

Light Bomber
DORNIER DO-217

GERMAN
ARMY

LIGHT BOMBER HENSCHEL HS–124

Description: Elliptical tip, slightly tapered, midwing
                 monoplane, inclosed cockpit, twin en-
                 gines, short rounded nose, engine na-
                 celles under wing, twin rudders, retract-
                 able landing gear.
Crew:
Armament: One cannon and two machine guns.
Ammunition:
Bomb load: 2,200 pounds.
Radio:
Armor:
Motors: Two 880-horsepower BMW 132 DC.
Maximum speed: 270 miles per hour.
Rate of climb:
Service ceiling:
Maximum range: 1,000 miles with 2,200 pounds.
Wing span:

Light Bomber
HENSCHEL HS-124

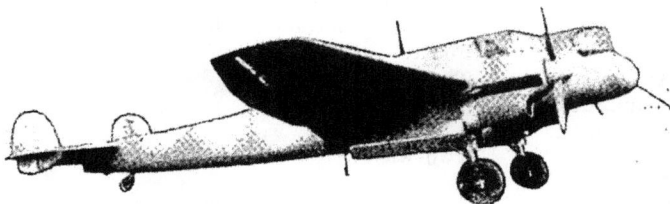

GERMAN
ARMY

LIGHT BOMBER JUNKERS JU–86K

Description: Square tip, swept-back, tapered, slightly dihedral, low-wing monoplane, inclosed cockpit, twin engines, long elliptical nose, engine nacelles set into wing, twin rudders, retractable landing gear.

Crew: Four.

Armament: Three machine guns.

Ammunition:

Bomb load: 2,200 pounds.

Radio: Two-way.

Armor:

Motors: Two 880-horsepower BMW 132.

Maximum speed: 248 miles per hour at 9,800 feet.

Rate of climb: 13,120 feet in 16 minutes.

Service ceiling: 24,000 feet.

Maximum range: 1,242 miles with 2,200 pounds.

Wing span: 73 feet 10 inches.

Light Bomber
JUNKERS JU–86K

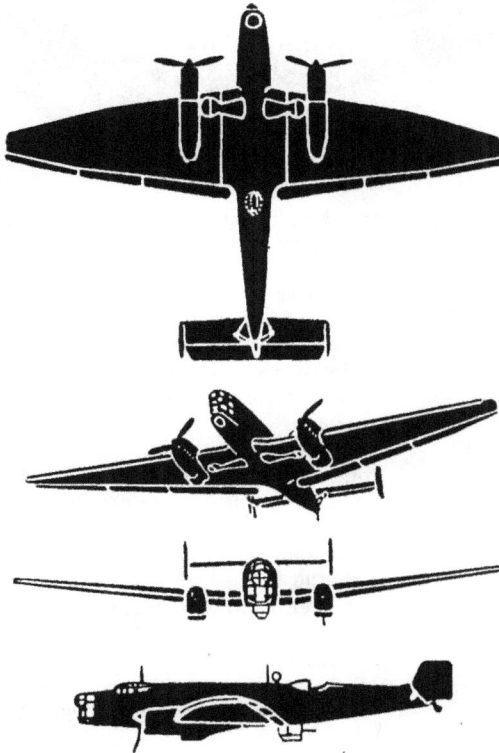

GERMAN
ARMY

LIGHT BOMBER MESSERSCHMITT JAGUAR
(SIMILAR TO ME–110)

Description: Long, narrow, slightly swept-back and ta-pered, low-wing monoplane, two midwing motors, pointed engine nacelles, in-closed cockpit, retractable landing gear, twin rudder fins and semiretractable tail wheel.

Crew: Two or three.

Armament: Four machine guns, fixed fuselage; two machine guns, flexible fuselage, rear; two 20-mm cannon, fixed nose.

Ammunition: 5,000 rounds per machine gun; 400 rounds per 20-mm.

Bomb load: Has been known to carry two 1,100-pound bombs.

Radio: Two-way and blind landing equipment.

Armor: Substantial armor plate.

Motors: Two 1,175-horsepower Daimler Benz, DB 601 motors.

Maximum speed: 320 miles per hour (estimate).

Rate of climb: 10,000 feet in 4.1 minutes; 20,000 feet in 10.1 minutes.

Service ceiling:

Maximum range: 2,000 miles.

Wing span: 55 feet.

Light Bomber
MESSERSCHMITT JAGUAR

49

GERMAN
ARMY

MEDIUM BOMBER HEINKEL HE–111K MK III

Description:	Elliptical, rounded, trailing edge, slight cutout, slightly dihedral, low-wing monoplane, twin midwing motors, pointed engine nacelles, long pointed nose, elliptical tail, and retractable landing gear.
Crew:	Five.
Armament:	Five machine guns.
Ammunition:	500 rounds per machine gun.
Bomb load:	2,200 to 4,500 pounds.
Radio:	Two-way.
Armor:	Self-seal tank; some crew protection.
Motors:	Two Junkers Jumo 211A, 1,200-horsepower.
Maximum speed:	261 miles per hour.
Rate of climb:	3,280 feet in 2.1 minutes.
Service ceiling:	24,100 feet.
Maximum range:	2,110 miles.
Wing span:	76 feet.

Medium Bomber
HEINKEL HE–111K MK III

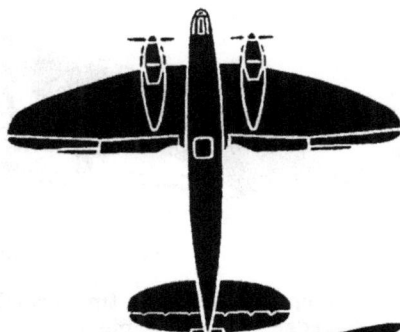

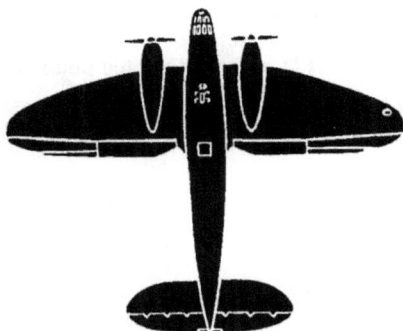

GERMAN
ARMY

MEDIUM BOMBER HEINKEL HE–111K MK V

Description :   Swept-back, round tip, straight, trailing
                       edge, low-wing monoplane, all metal,
                       twin midwing motors, pointed engine
                       nacelles, short nose, retractable landing
                       gear and tail wheel, elliptical tail plane,
                       and gun turrets showing above and below
                       fuselage.
Crew: Four.
Armament: Three 50-mm machine guns or cannon in
                       nose, top of fuselage, and dust bin.
Ammunition: 500 rounds per machine gun.
Bomb load: 4.400 pounds.
Radio: Two-way.
Armor:
Motors: Two 1,150-horsepower DB 601A.
Maximum speed: 274 miles per hour at 12,300 feet.
Rate of climb: To 13,120 feet in 16.8 minutes.
Service ceiling: 24,100 feet.
Maximum range: 2,170 miles with 4,400 pounds.
Wing span: 76 feet.

Medium Bomber
HEINKEL HE–111K MK V

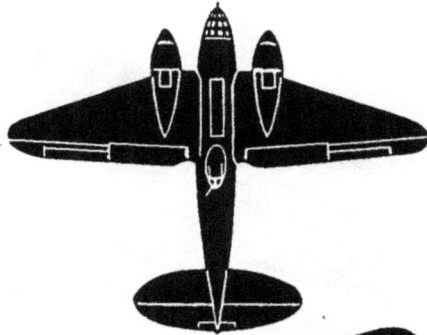

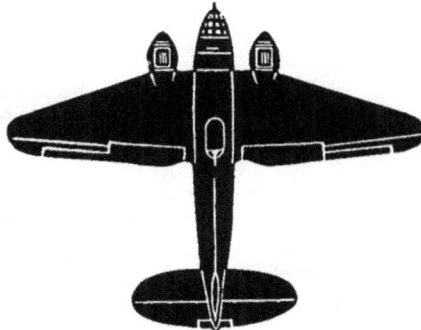

GERMAN
ARMY

MEDIUM BOMBER HEINKEL HE–111K MK. VA

Description:	Slightly swept-back, tapered, round tip, slightly dihedral, low-wing monoplane, all metal, twin midwing motors, pointed engine nacelles, short nose, retractable landing gear and tail wheel, and elliptical tail plane.
Crew:	Four.
Armament:	Three flexible 50-mm machine guns or cannon in nose, top of fuselage, and dust bin.
Ammunition:	
Bomb load:	Four 1,100-pound.
Radio:	Two-way.
Armor:	
Motors:	Two 1,200-horsepower Jumo 211A.
Maximum speed:	280 miles per hour at 14,000 feet.
Rate of climb:	To 13,120 feet in 17 minutes.
Service ceiling:	26,200 feet.
Maximum range:	2,110 miles at cruising speed with 2,200-pound bomb load or 2,640 miles without load.
Wing span:	74 feet.

Medium Bomber
HEINKEL HE–111K MK VA

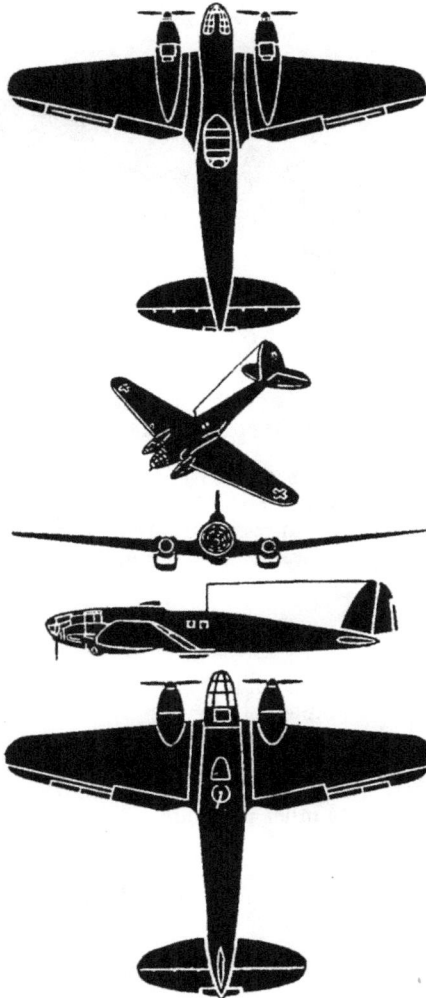

GERMAN
ARMY

MEDIUM BOMBER HEINKEL HE–111, SERIES H

Description: Round tip, tapered, slightly dihedral, mid-wing monoplane, inclosed cockpit, twin engines, transparent nose, engine nacelles set into wing, retractable landing gear.

Crew:

Armament: Five machine guns.

Ammunition:

Bomb load: 4,400 pounds.

Radio: Complete.

Armor: Self-seal tank; back and top of pilot's compartment.

Motors: Two 1,200-horsepower Junkers Juno 211D.

Maximum speed: 274 miles per hour.

Rate of climb:

Service ceiling:

Maximum range: 2,140 miles at 230 miles per hour.

Wing span:

Medium Bomber
HEINKEL HE–111
SERIES H

GERMAN
ARMY

HEAVY BOMBER DORNIER DO-19
(Obsolescent)

Description:	Round tip, tapered, slightly swept-back, dihedral, low-wing monoplane, inclosed cockpit, four engines, long rounded nose, retractable landing gear.
Crew:	Six.
Armament:	Four machine guns.
Ammunition:	
Bomb load:	
Radio:	
Armor:	
Motors:	Four 650-horsepower Bramo 322 H-2.
Maximum speed:	236 miles per hour at 13,100 feet.
Rate of climb:	
Service ceiling:	
Maximum range:	
Wing span:	105 feet.

Heavy Bomber
DORNIER DO–19

GERMAN
ARMY

HEAVY BOMBER FOCKE-WULF FW-200 (CONDOR)

Description:	Slightly swept-back, tapered, round tip, slightly dihedral, four-motor monoplane, blunt engine nacelles, long pointed nose, elliptical tail plane, and retractable landing gear and tail wheel.
Crew:	Six.
Armament:	Cannon and machine guns.
Ammunition:	
Bomb load:	5,200 pounds; or 30 troops.
Radio:	Code two-way and VH.
Armor:	
Motors:	Four 950-horsepower BMW 132.
Maximum speed:	259 miles per hour at 9,500 feet.
Rate of climb:	To 3,280 feet in 2.5 minutes; to 13,120 feet in 14.3 minutes.
Service ceiling:	28,000 feet.
Maximum range:	775 to 1,180 miles, depending on gasoline and bomb load.
Wing span:	108 feet.

Heavy Bömber
FOCKE-WULF FW–200

GERMAN
ARMY

HEAVY BOMBER FOCKE-WULF KURIER

Description:	Slightly swept-back, tapered, round tip, slightly dihedral, 4-motor monoplane, blunt engine nacelles, long pointed nose, elliptical tail plane, and retractable landing gear and tail wheel. (Similar to Focke-Wulf Fw-200 Condor.)
Crew:	Six.
Armament:	One cannon and eight machine guns.
Ammunition:	
Bomb load:	6,600 pounds.
Radio:	Code two-way and VH.
Armor:	10-mm plate full armor.
Motors:	Four 1,300-horsepower BMW 801.
Maximum speed:	265 miles per hour at 9,500 feet.
Rate of climb:	To 3,280 feet in 2.5 minutes; to 13,120 feet in 14.3 minutes.
Service ceiling:	28,000 feet.
Maximum range:	3,000 miles.
Wing span:	108 feet.

Heavy Bomber
FOCKE-WULF KURIER

GERMAN
ARMY

HEAVY BOMBER HEINKEL HE–177

Description:	Sharp taper, four-engine, heavy bomber, midwing monoplane, wings well back from nose, all metal; exceptionally thick wing.
Crew:	Five.
Armament:	Five machine guns; cannon are contemplated.
Ammunition:	6,000 rounds total.
Bomb load:	12,000 pounds, normal.
Radio:	Two-way.
Armor:	Armor protection for rear gunner.
Motors:	Four 1,325-horsepower DB 606.
Maximum speed:	340 miles per hour.
Rate of climb:	20,000 feet in 30 minutes
Service ceiling:	26,000 feet.
Maximum range:	3,400 miles.
Wing span:	103 feet.

Heavy Bomber
HEINKEL HE–177

GERMAN
ARMY

HEAVY BOMBER JUNKERS JU–89

Description:	All metal, low-wing monoplane, retractable landing gear.
Crew:	Six.
Armament:	Two cannon and two machine guns.
Ammunition:	
Bomb load:	7,938 pounds.
Radio:	Two-way.
Armor:	
Motors:	Four 1,000-horsepower Junkers Jumo 211.
Maximum speed:	270 miles per hour.
Rate of climb:	
Service ceiling:	33,951 feet.
Maximum range:	1,491 miles.
Wing span:	115 feet.

Heavy Bomber
JUNKERS JU–89

GERMAN
ARMY

HEAVY BOMBER JUNKERS JU-90

Description:	Extremely swept-back, square tip, slightly dihedral, low-wing cabin monoplane, four midwing motors, blunt engine nacelles, long pointed nose, retractable landing gear, and twin rudder fins.
Crew:	Three.
Armament:	
Ammunition:	
Troop capacity:	Forty.
Bomb load:	
Radio:	
Armor:	
Motors:	Four 830-horsepower BMW 132H.
Maximum speed:	217 miles per hour.
Rate of climb:	
Service ceiling:	18,040 feet.
Maximum range:	1,300 miles.
Wing span:	115 feet.

Heavy Bomber
JUNKERS JU–90

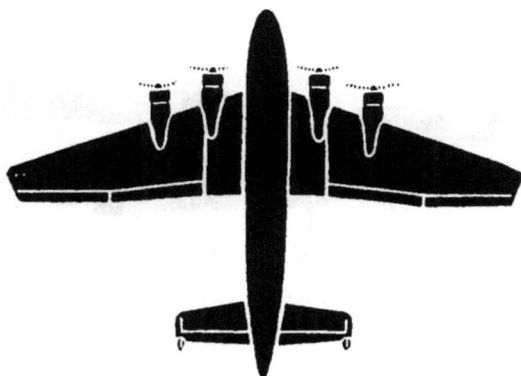

GERMAN
ARMY

OBSERVATION FIESELER FI–156 "STORCH"

Description: High-wing, braced-wing, monoplane, fuse-
                    lage steel tubing and fabric, wings wood
                    and fabric, fixed landing gear.
Crew: Three.
Armament:
Ammunition:
Bomb load:
Radio: Two-way code, low power.
Armor:
Motors: One 240-horsepower Argus As 10c 3, air-
                    cooled.
Maximum speed: 108 miles per hour; landing speed 25 miles
                    per hour.
Rate of climb: 6,560 feet in 8.8 minutes.
Service ceiling: 17,000 feet.
Maximum range: 247 miles.
Wing span: 47 feet.

Observation
FIESELER FI–156 "STORCH"

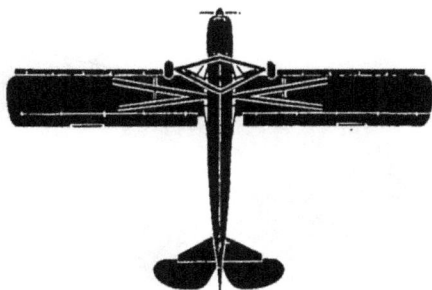

GERMAN ARMY

OBSERVATION HENSCHEL HS–126

Description:	Swept-back, round tip, rounded trailing edge with cut-out, parasol monoplane, single-motor, blunt nose, and fixed landing gear.
Crew:	Two.
Armament:	Two machine guns.
Ammunition:	500 rounds for front gun; 975 rounds for rear gun.
Bomb load:	Ten 22-pound.
Radio:	Code two-way-M.
Armor:	
Motors:	One 870-horsepower BMW 132 DC, air-cooled.
Maximum speed:	230 miles per hour at 16,400 feet.
Rate of climb:	To 6,560 feet in 3.5 minutes; to 19,700 feet in 11.7 minutes.
Service ceiling:	27,880 feet.
Maximum range:	620 miles.
Wing span:	48 feet.

Observation
HENSCHEL HS–126

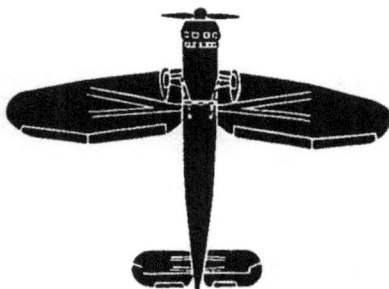

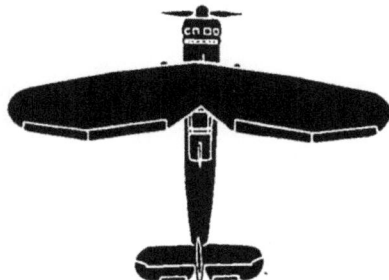

GERMAN
ARMY

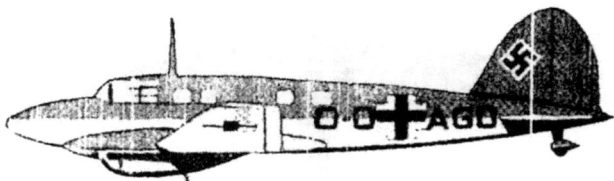

LIGHT TRANSPORT AGO AO–192 KURIER
(Obsolescent)

Description:	Square tip, swept-back, dihedra:., low-wing monoplane, inclosed cockpit, twin engines, long pointed nose, engine nacelles set into the wing, retractable landing gear.
Crew:	Two.
Armament:	
Ammunition:	
Passenger load:	Six.
Bomb load:	
Radio:	
Armor:	
Motors:	Two 240-horsepower Hirth HM 509D.
Maximum speed:	208 miles per hour.
Rate of climb:	
Service ceiling:	16,400 feet.
Maximum range:	650 miles at 171 miles per hour.
Wing span:	45 feet.

Light Transport
AGO AO–192 KURIER
(Obsolescent)

GERMAN
ARMY

TROOP TRANSPORT BLOHM AND VOSS HA-142

Description:	Slightly rounded tip, rather straight negative dihedral, inclosed cockpit, four engines, long rounded nose, engine nacelles set into the wing, twin rudders, retractable landing gear.
Crew:	Four.
Armament:	
Ammunition:	
Bomb load:	
Radio:	
Armor:	
Motors:	Four 880-horsepower BMW 132H.
Maximum speed:	248 miles per hour.
Rate of climb:	3,280 feet in 2.5 minutes.
Service ceiling:	22,305 feet.
Maximum range:	2,732 miles at 217 miles per hour.
Wing span:	97 feet.

Troop Transport
BLOHM AND VOSS HA–142

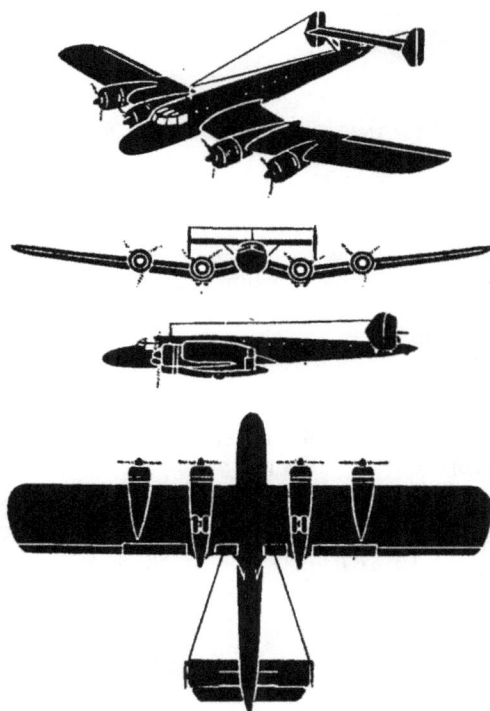

GERMAN
ARMY

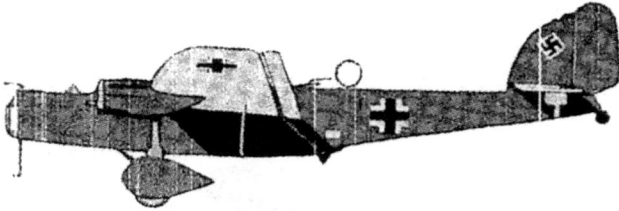

TRANSPORT DORNIER DO-23

Description:	Square tip, slightly swept-back, dihedral, midwing monoplane, long elliptical nose, twin engines, fixed landing gear.
Crew:	Four.
Armament:	Three machine guns.
Ammunition:	
Passenger load:	
Bomb load:	
Radio:	
Armor:	
Motors:	Two 750-horsepower BMW VIu.
Maximum speed:	161 miles per hour.
Rate of climb:	886 feet per minute.
Service ceiling:	13,776 feet.
Maximum range:	930 miles at 130 miles per hour.
Wing span:	84 feet.

Transport
DORNIER DO–23

GERMAN
ARMY

TROOP TRANSPORT JUNKERS JU–52

Description:	Swept-back, tapered, square tip, slightly dihedral, low-wing monoplane, three motors, blunt engine nacelles, and fixed landing gear.
Crew:	Three.
Armament:	One machine gun.
Ammunition:	
Troop capacity:	Fifteen men with full equipment.
Bomb load:	
Radio:	Yes.
Armor:	
Motors:	Three 870-horsepower BMW 132 DC, air-cooled.
Maximum speed:	120 miles per hour at cruising speed.
Rate of climb:	
Service ceiling:	
Maximum range:	
Wing span:	

Troop Transport
JUNKERS JU–52

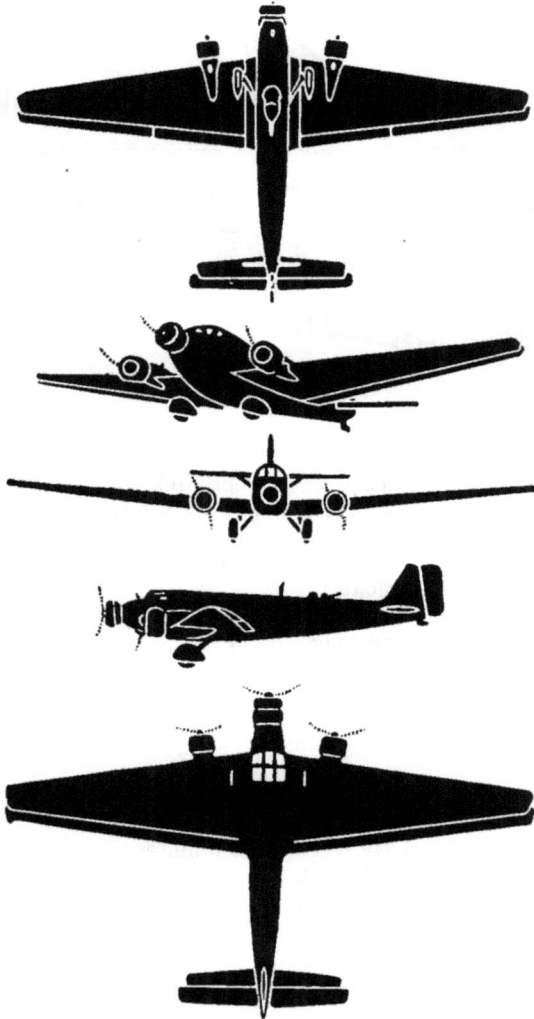

GERMAN
ARMY

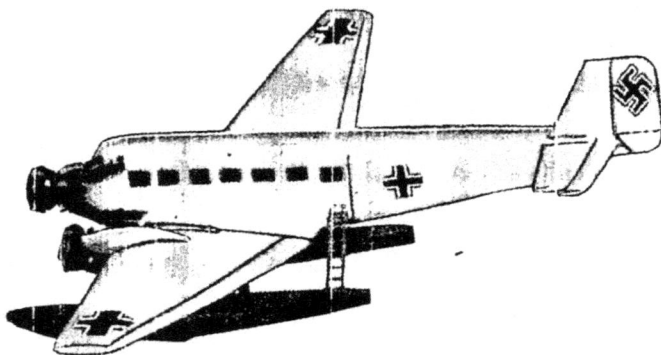

TROOP TRANSPORT JUNKERS JU–52/3M W

Description:	Square tip, swept-back, tapered, slightly dihedral, low-wing monoplane, inclosed cabin, three engines, fixed landing gear. This model may be equipped with twin floats.
Crew:	
Armament:	Two machine guns.
Ammunition:	
Troop capacity:	Twenty.
Bomb load:	
Radio:	
Armor:	
Motors:	Three 960-horsepower BMW 13?.
Maximum speed:	175 miles per hour.
Rate of climb:	9,840 feet in 17.5 minutes.
Service ceiling:	20,000 feet.
Maximum range:	1,000 miles.
Wing span:	96 feet.

Troop Transport
JUNKERS JU–52/3M W

**GERMAN
ARMY**

TRANSPORT GLIDER

Description: Round tip, slightly tapered, high-wing,
               parasol type, inclosed cabin.

Crew:

Armament:

Ammunition:

Troop capacity: Twelve to fifteen men.

Bomb load:

Radio:

Armor:

Motors:

Maximum speed:

Rate of climb:

Service ceiling:

Maximum range:

Wing span: 80 feet.

Transport
GLIDER

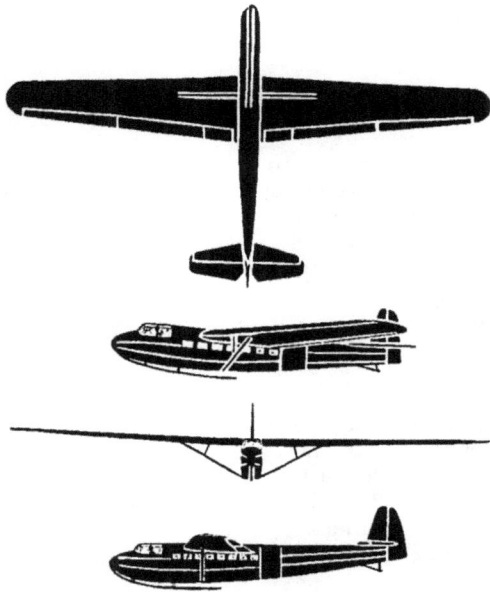

GERMAN
ARMY

TRAINER ARADO AR–68G
(Obsolescent)

Description: Round tip, straight-wing biplane, stag-
                   gered, open cockpit, single-engine, fixed
                   landing gear.
Crew: One.
Armament: Two fixed forward-firing machine guns.
Ammunition:
Bomb load:
Radio:
Armor:
Motors: One 750-horsepower BMW VI.
Maximum speed: 205 miles per hour.
Rate of climb: 1,200 feet per minute.
Service ceiling: 24,200 feet.
Maximum range: 310 miles at 180 miles per hour.
Wing span: 36 feet.

Trainer
ARADO AR–68G

GERMAN
ARMY

TRAINER ARADO AR-77
(Obsolescent)

Description: Round tip, tapered, dihedral, low-wing monoplane, inclosed cockpit, twin engines, engine nacelles below wings, fixed landing gear.

Crew: Four or five.

Armament:

Ammunition:

Bomb load:

Radio:

Armor:

Motors: Two 240-horsepower Argus As 10c.

Maximum speed: 152 miles per hour.

Rate of climb: 783 feet per minute.

Service ceiling: 15,200 feet.

Maximum range: 447 miles at 125 miles per hour.

Wing span: 59 feet.

IDENTIFICATION OF GERMAN AIRCRAFT

Trainer
ARADO AR–77

GERMAN
ARMY

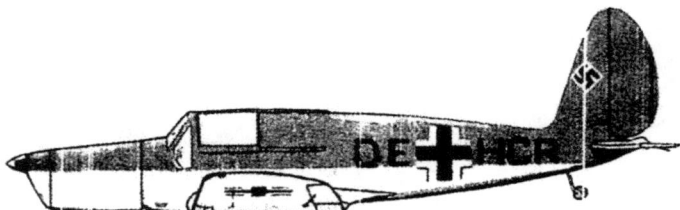

TRAINER ARADO AR–79

Description:	Round tip, slightly swept-back, slightly tapered, negative dihedral, inclosed cockpit, single-engine, long tapered nose, retractable landing gear
Crew:	Two.
Armament:	
Ammunition:	
Bomb load:	
Radio:	
Armor:	
Motors:	One 105-horsepower Hirth HM 504 A2.
Maximum speed:	143 miles per hour.
Rate of climb:	1,020 feet per minute.
Service ceiling:	18,040 feet.
Maximum range:	636 miles at 127 miles per hour.
Wing span:	33 feet.

IDENTIFICATION OF GERMAN AIRCRAFT

Trainer
ARADO AR–79

GERMAN
ARMY

TRAINER ARADO AR–96
(Obsolescent)

Description:	Slightly rounded tip, swept-back, dihedral, low-wing monoplane, inclosed cockpit, single-engine, retractable landing gear.
Crew:	Two.
Armament:	
Ammunition:	
Bomb load:	
Radio:	
Armor:	
Motors:	One 240-horsepower Argus As 10c.
Maximum speed:	183 miles per hour.
Rate of climb:	1,250 feet per minute.
Service ceiling:	15,090 feet.
Maximum range:	490 miles at 149 miles per hour.
Wing span:	36 feet

Trainer
ARADO AR–96

GERMAN
ARMY

TRAINER ARADO. AR–96B

Description: Slightly rounded tip, swept-back, dihedral,
                    low-wing monoplane, inclosed cockpit,
                    single-engine, retractable landing gear.
Crew: Two.
Armament:
Ammunition:
Bomb load:
Radio:
Armor:
Motors: One 450-horsepower Argus As 410A.
Maximum speed: 211 miles per hour.
Rate of climb: 1,320 feet per minute.
Service ceiling: 23,616 feet.
Maximum range: 685 miles at 171 miles per hour.
Wing span: 36 feet.

IDENTIFICATION OF GERMAN AIRCRAFT

Trainer
ARADO AR–96B

95

**GERMAN
ARMY**

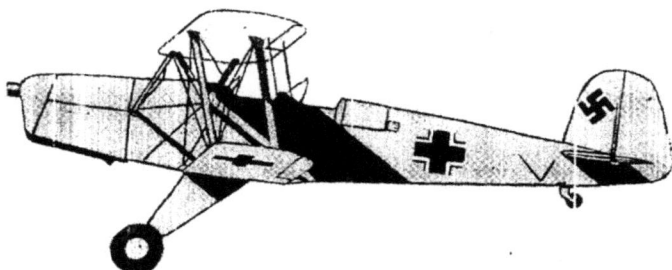

TRAINER BÜCKER BÜ–131B JUNGMANN

Description:	Round tip, straight-wing, staggered bi-plane, open cockpit, single-engine, fixed landing gear.
Crew:	Two.
Armament:	
Ammunition:	
Bomb load:	
Radio:	
Armor:	
Motors:	One 100-horsepower Hirth HM 504.
Maximum speed:	115 miles per hour.
Rate of climb:	590 feet per minute.
Service ceiling:	14,000 feet.
Maximum range:	500 miles at 106 miles per hour.
Wing span:	24 feet.

Trainer
BÜCKER BÜ–131B JUNGMANN

GERMAN
ARMY

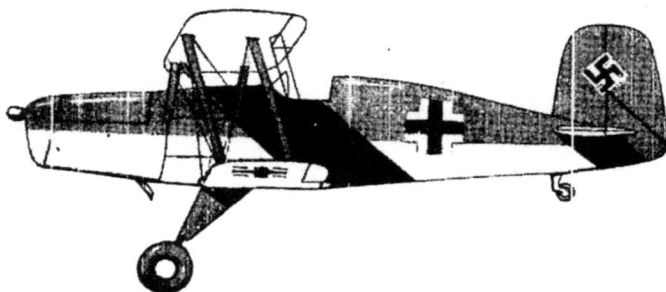

TRAINER BÜCKER BÜ–133C JUNGMEISTER (IN LINE)

Description: Round tip, straight-wing, staggered bi-
                 plane, open cockpit, single engine, long
                 tapered nose, fixed landing gear.
Crew: One.
Armament:
Ammunition:
Bomb load:
Radio:
Armor:
Motors: One 140-horsepower Hirth HM 506.
Maximum speed: 115 miles per hour.
Rate of climb: 630 feet per minute.
Service ceiling: 14,000 feet.
Maximum range: 400 miles at 106 miles per hour.
Wing span: 22 feet.

Trainer
BÜCKER BÜ–133C JUNGMEISTER
(IN LINE)

GERMAN
ARMY

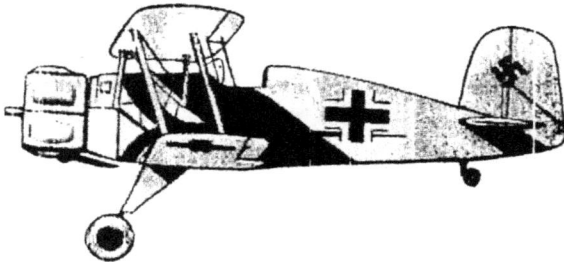

TRAINER BÜCKER BÜ–133C JUNGMEISTER (RADIAL)

Description:	Round tip, straight-wing, staggered bi-plane, oper. cockpit, single radial engine, blunt nose, fixed landing gear.
Crew:	One.
Armament:	
Ammunition:	
Bomb load:	
Radio:	
Armor:	
Motors:	One 160-horsepower Siemens Sh 14 A–4.
Maximum speed:	134 miles per hour.
Rate of climb:	1,170 feet per minute.
Service ceiling:	20,000 feet.
Maximum range:	310 miles at 125 miles per hour.
Wing span:	22 feet.

Trainer
BÜCKER BÜ–133C JUNGMEISTER
(RADIAL)

GERMAN
ARMY

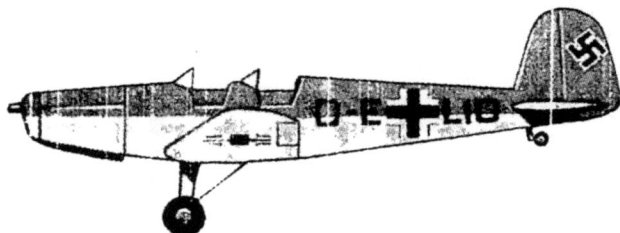

TRAINER BÜCKER BÜ–180 STUDENT

Description:	Slightly rounded tip, swept-back, dihedral, low-wing monoplane, open cockpit, single-engine, long tapered nose, fixed landing gear.
Crew:	Two.
Armament:	
Ammunition:	
Bomb load:	
Radio:	
Armor:	
Motors:	One 60-horsepower Walter Mikron II.
Maximum speed:	108 miles per hour.
Rate of climb:	505 feet per minute.
Service ceiling:	13,100 feet.
Maximum range:	400 miles at 99 miles per hour.
Wing span:	38 feet.

Trainer
BÜCKER BÜ–180 STUDENT

GERMAN
ARMY

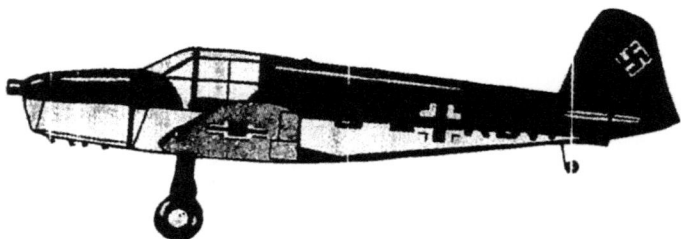

TRAINER BÜCKER BÜ–181 BESTMANN

Description:	Slightly rounded tip, swept-back, dihedral, low-wing monoplane, inclosed cockpit, single-engine, long tapered nose, fixed landing gear.
Crew:	Two.
Armament:	
Ammunition:	
Bomb load:	
Radio:	
Armor:	
Motors:	One 85-horsepower Hirth HM 504.
Maximum speed:	133 miles per hour.
Rate of climb:	620 feet per minute.
Service ceiling:	16,400 feet.
Maximum range:	500 miles at 120 miles per hour.
Wing span:	35 feet.

Trainer
BÜCKER BÜ–181 BESTMANN

GERMAN
ARMY

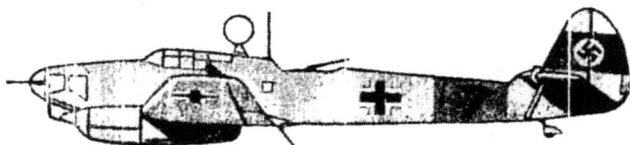

TRAINER FOCKE-WULF FW–58W, WEIHE

Description:	Round tip, swept-back, tapered, dihedral, low-wing monoplane, inclosed cockpit, twin engines, nacelles set beneath wing, transparent nose, retractable landing gear.
Crew:	Four.
Armament:	One flexible forward and one flexible rear, machine gun.
Ammunition:	
Bomb load:	
Radio:	
Armor:	
Motors:	Two 240-horsepower, Argus As 10c.
Maximum speed:	158 miles per hour.
Rate of climb:	1,000 feet in 1 minute.
Service ceiling:	17,700 feet.
Maximum range:	465 miles.
Wing span:	69 feet.

Trainer
FOCKE-WULF FW–58W, WEIHE

GERMAN
ARMY

TRAINER GOTHA GO–145B

Description: Round tip, straight-wing biplane, staggered, open cockpit, single-engine, long tapered nose, fixed landing gear.

Crew: Two.

Armament: One fixed forward and one flexible rear, machine gun.

Ammunition:

Bomb load:

Radio:

Armor:

Motors: One 240-horsepower Argus As 10c.

Maximum speed: 132 miles per hour.

Rate of climb:

Service ceiling: 12,140 feet.

Maximum range: 400 miles.

Wing span: 30 feet.

Trainer
GOTHA GO–145B

NAVY AIRCRAFT

GERMAN
NAVY

PATROL BLOHM AND VOSS HA–138

Description:	Tapered, round tip monoplane flying boat, three motors, floats attached to under-surface of wings, and twin boom tail.
Crew:	Four.
Armament:	4 machine guns; retractable gun turret in nose and gun positions behind middle motor and in stern of short hull.
Ammunition:	
Bomb load:	
Radio:	
Armor:	
Motors:	Three 600-horsepower Junkers Jumo 205c Diesel motors.
Maximum speed:	171 miles per hour.
Rate of climb:	13,128 feet in 48 minutes.
Service ceiling:	
Maximum range:	1,500 miles at 146 miles per hour.
Wing span:	89 feet.

Patrol
BLOHM AND VOSS HA–138

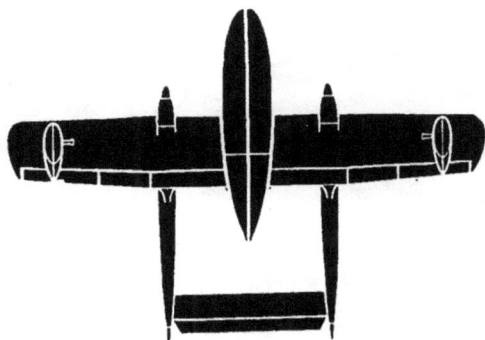

GERMAN
NAVY

PATROL DORNIER DO–18K

Description:	Slightly swept-back, slightly tapered, round tip monoplane flying boat, twin motors in tandem, sponsons or sea wings protruding from the hull of the float and braced to the wing.
Crew:	Four.
Armament:	Three machine guns.
Ammunition:	
Bomb load:	2,200 pounds.
Radio:	Yes.
Armor:	
Motors:	Two 750-horsepower Jumo 205.
Maximum speed:	155 miles per hour.
Rate of climb:	
Service ceiling:	18,370 feet.
Maximum range:	3,600 miles.
Wing span:	86 feet.

Patrol
DORNIER DO–18K

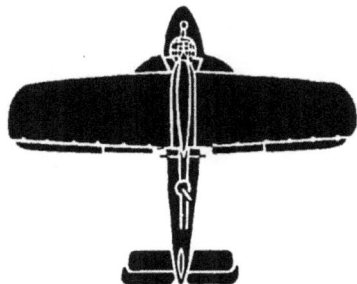

GERMAN
NAVY

PATROL DORNIER DO-26

Description:	High-wing monoplane flying boat, four motors with engine nacelles protruding above the wings, two each in tandem.
Crew:	Six.
Armament:	Gun turret in nose and one behind wing.
Ammunition:	
Bomb load:	2,000 pounds.
Radio:	Yes.
Armor:	
Motors:	Four 750-horsepower Jumo 205c Diesel motors.
Maximum speed:	208 miles per hour.
Rate of climb:	
Service ceiling:	
Maximum range:	5,600 miles at 190 miles per hour.
Wing span:	99 feet.

Patrol
DORNIER DO–26

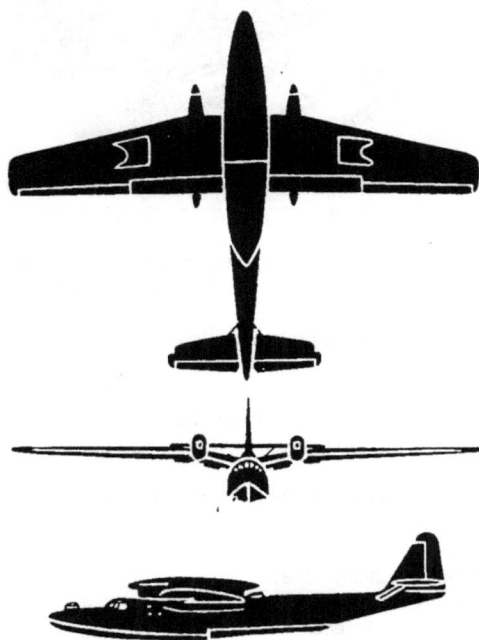

GERMAN
NAVY

TORPEDO BOMBER ARADO AR–95W

Description:	Swept-back, round tip biplane, twin float seaplane, single-motor, and blunt nose.
Crew:	Two or three.
Armament:	Two machine guns.
Ammunition:	500 rounds (front); 750 (rear).
Bomb load:	Six 110-pound, one 1,760-pound torpedo, or 825-pound smoke tank.
Radio:	Two-way.
Armor:	
Motors:	One 880-horsepower BMW 132 DC.
Maximum speed:	204 miles per hour.
Rate of climb:	To 13,120 feet in 7.6 minutes.
Service ceiling:	25,580 feet.
Maximum range:	1,026 miles.
Wing span:	41 feet.

Torpedo Bomber
ARADO AR–95W

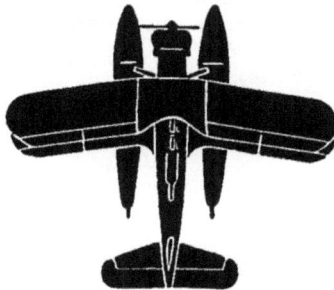

119

GERMAN
NAVY

TORPEDO BOMBER BLOHM AND VOSS HA-140

Description:	Round tip, slightly dihedral, midwing monoplane, twin float seaplane, twin midwing motors, blunt engine nacelles, and twin rudder fins.
Crew:	Four.
Armament:	Two machine guns. Torpedo or bombs.
Ammunition:	
Bomb load:	1,760-pound torpedo.
Radio:	
Armor:	
Motors:	Two 880-horsepower BMW 132 DC.
Maximum speed:	199 miles per hour.
Rate of climb:	9,840 feet in 11.5 minutes.
Service ceiling:	16,400 feet.
Maximum range:	1,240 miles with torpedo; 1,550 miles on patrol.
Wing span:	69 feet.

Torpedo Bomber
BLOHM AND VOSS HA–140

GERMAN
NAVY

TORPEDO BOMBER FIESELER FI-167

Description: All metal biplane, single liquid-cooled mo-
                    tor, pointed nose, and fixed landing gear;
                    for operation from carrier.
Crew: Two.
Armament: Two guns. One torpedo.
Ammunition:
Bomb load: One 2,200-pound torpedo or two 1,100-
                    pound bombs; four 550-pound.
Radio:
Armor:
Motors: 1,150-horsepower DB 601B.
Maximum speed: 202 miles per hour at 12,100 feet.
Rate of climb:
Service ceiling: 26,900 feet.
Maximum range: 930 miles; when fully loaded, 404 miles.
Wing span: 44 feet.

Torpedo Bomber
FIESELER FI–167

GERMAN
NAVY

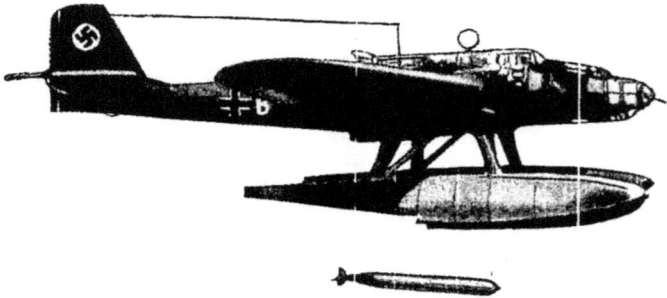

TORPEDO BOMBER HEINKEL HE–115

Description:	Swept-back, tapered, round tip, midwing monoplane, twin float seaplane, twin midwing motors, and blunt engine nacelles.
Crew:	Two.
Armament:	Two machine guns and one cannon.
Ammunition:	Boxes and their housings would accommodate ammunition up to 174 millimeters long.
Bomb load:	2,200 pounds bombs, mines, or torpedo.
Radio:	Two-way.
Armor:	14-mm panel fitted behind pilot's head and shoulders.
Motors:	Two 850-horsepower BMW 132N.
Maximum speed:	221 miles per hour.
Rate of climb:	6,600 feet in 8.5 minutes.
Service ceiling:	21,300 feet.
Maximum range:	1,300 miles.
Wing span:	73 feet.

Torpedo Bomber
HEINKEL HE–115

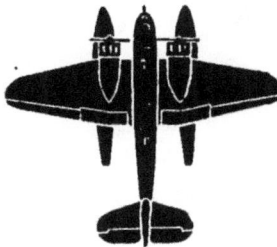

GERMAN
NAVY

PATROL BOMBER ARADO AR–196

Description:	Slightly rounded tip, straight-wing, dihe-drai, low-wing monoplane, inclosed cock-pit, single-engine, blunt nose, with twin floats.
Crew:	Two.
Armament:	Two machine guns.
Ammunition:	
Bomb load:	Six 110-pound bombs or one 1,760-pound bomb.
Radio:	
Armor:	
Motors:	One 900-horsepower Bramo Fafnir.
Maximum speed:	190 miles per hour.
Rate of climb:	3,280 feet in 4.6 minutes.
Service ceiling:	17,056 feet.
Maximum range:	502 miles.
Wing span:	36 feet.

Patrol Bomber
ARADO AR–196

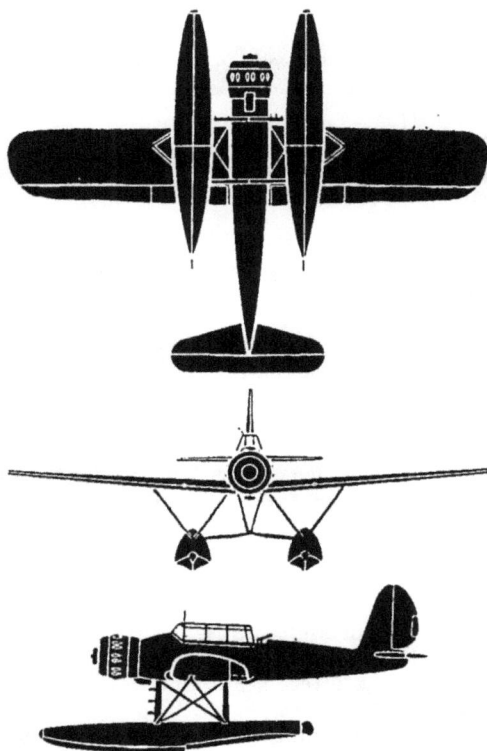

GERMAN
NAVY

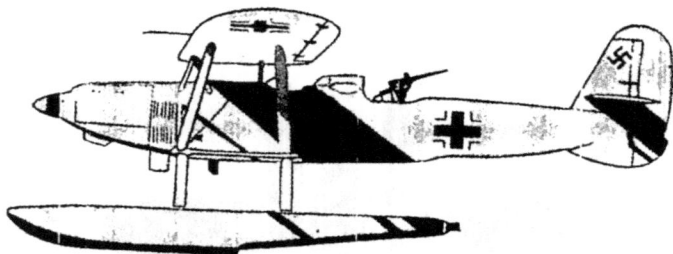

PATROL BOMBER DORNIER DO–22
(Obsolescent)

Description:	Round tip, straight-wing, high-wing monoplane, parasol type, open cockpit, single-engine, long tapered nose, with fixed floats.
Crew:	Three.
Armament:	One fixed machine gun forward and two flexible machine guns.
Ammunition:	
Bomb load:	
Radio:	
Armor:	
Motors:	One Mercedes Benz DB 600G.
Maximum speed:	217 miles per hour.
Rate of climb:	1,260 feet per minute.
Service ceiling:	30,180 feet.
Maximum range:	1,430 miles at 186 miles per hour.
Wing span:	53 feet.

Patrol Bomber
DORNIER DO–22

GERMAN
NAVY

PATROL BOMBER DORNIER DO-24

Description:	Swept-back, round tip monoplane, flying boat, blunt engine nacelles, sponsons or sea wings of hull braced to wings, three midwing motors, and twin rudder fins.
Crew:	Five.
Armament:	Three flexible machine guns.
Ammunition:	
Bomb load:	3,300 pounds.
Radio:	Two-way code and voice.
Armor:	
Motors:	Three 760-horsepower BMW 132 DC.
Maximum speed:	195 miles per hour.
Rate of climb:	To 3,250 feet in 3.5 minutes.
Service ceiling:	18,700 feet.
Maximum range:	2,175 miles.
Wing span:	89 feet.

Patrol Bomber
DORNIER DO–24

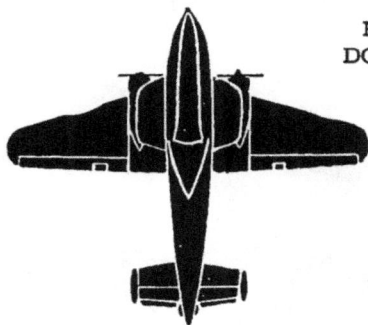

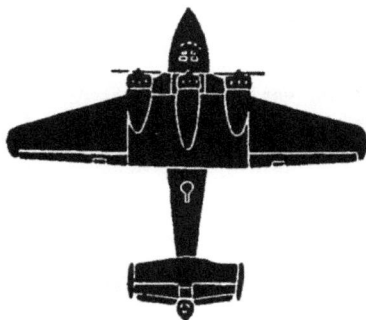

131

GERMAN
NAVY

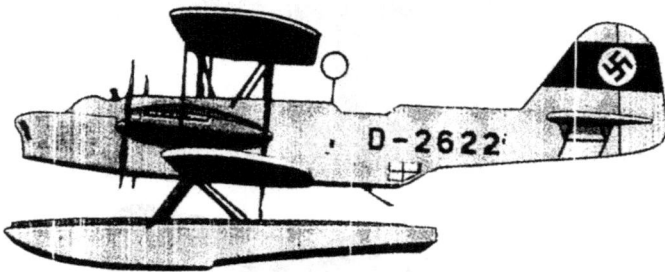

PATROL BOMBER HEINKEL HE–59

Description:	Straight, round tip biplane, twin float seaplane, twin motors, and pointed engine nacelles.
Crew:	Four.
Armament:	Three machine guns.
Ammunition:	
Bomb load:	1,760-pound torpedo; 2,200 pounds of bombs.
Radio:	Two-way code.
Armor:	
Motors:	Two 750-horsepower BMW VI.
Maximum speed:	140 miles per hour.
Rate of climb:	To 3,280 feet in 4.8 minutes.
Service ceiling:	
Maximum range:	1,088 miles.
Wing span:	78 feet.

Patrol Bomber
HEINKEL HE–59

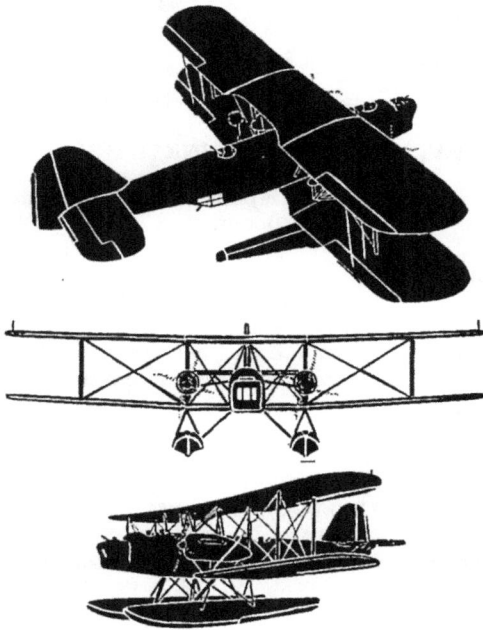

GERMAN
NAVY

PATROL BOMBER HEINKEL HE-114

Description:	Biplane seaplane, fuselage all metal, wings fabric, floats.
Crew:	Two.
Armament:	One fixed 7.9-mm machine gun in fuselage in front and one flexible machine gun in fuselage, rear.
Ammunition:	500 rounds per machine gun.
Bomb load:	Light bomb can be accommodated.
Radio:	Two-way code.
Armor:	
Motors:	One 880-horsepower BMW 132 DC.
Maximum speed:	205 miles per hour.
Rate of climb:	3,280 feet in 3 minutes.
Service ceiling:	23,000 feet.
Maximum range:	696 miles; 510 miles with bombs.
Wing span:	45 feet.

Patrol Bomber
HEINKEL HE–114

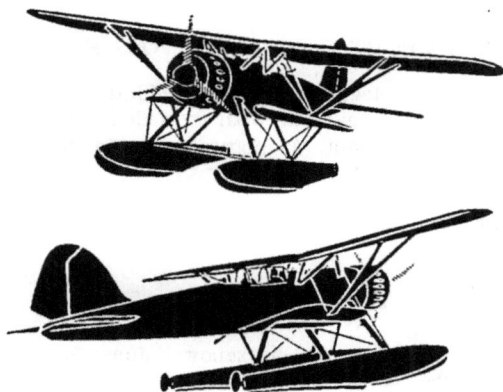

GERMAN
NAVY

TRANSPORT BLOHM AND VOSS HA–139

Description:	Negative dihedral, round tip monoplane, seaplane with twin floats, four midwing motors, pointed engine nacelles, and twin rudder fins.
Crew:	Four.
Armament:	Four machine guns.
Ammunition:	
Bomb load:	
Radio:	Yes.
Armor:	
Motors:	Four 650-horsepower Jumo 205.
Maximum speed:	200 miles per hour.
Rate of climb:	3,280 feet in 6 minutes.
Service ceiling:	14,100 feet.
Maximum range:	3,230 miles.
Wing span:	81 feet.

Transport
BLOHM AND VOSS HA–139

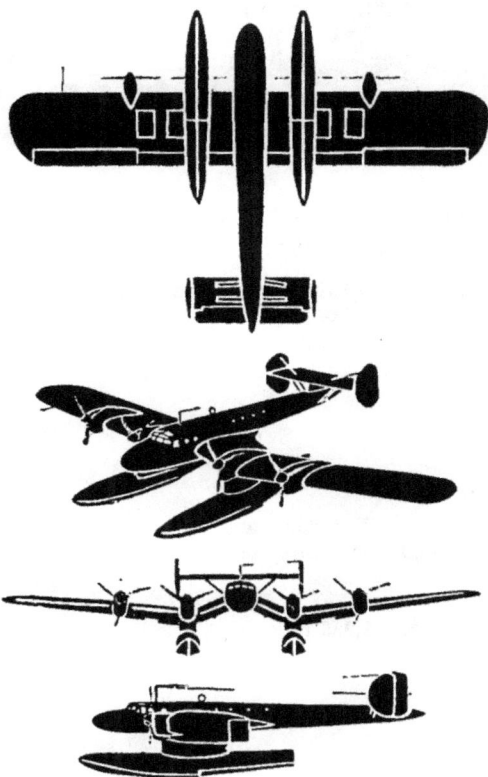

GERMAN
NAVY

TRANSPORT FLYING BOAT DORNIER WAL 1933/34
(Obsolescent)

Description: Straight-edged, straight biplane flying
                    boat, twin engines, nacelles above upper
                    wing, long pointed nose.
Crew: Three.
Armament:
Ammunition:
Bomb load:
Radio:
Armor:
Motors: Two 660-horsepower BMW VI.
Maximum speed: 143 miles per hour.
Rate of climb:
Service ceiling:
Maximum range: 2,230 miles at 130 miles per hour.
Wing span:

Transport Flying Boat
DORNIER WAL 1933/34

GERMAN
NAVY

TRAINER FOCKE-WULF FW-58W, WEIHE

Description:	Round tip, swept-back, tapered, dihedral, low-wing monoplane, inclosed cockpit, twin engines, nacelles set beneath wing, transparent nose, fixed floats.
Crew:	Four.
Armament:	One flexible forward and one flexible rear, machine gun.
Ammunition:	
Bomb load:	
Radio:	
Armor:	
Motors:	Two 240-horsepower Argus As 10c.
Maximum speed:	140 miles per hour.
Rate of climb:	670 feet per minute.
Service ceiling:	11,750 feet.
Maximum range:	540 miles.
Wing span:	69 feet.

www.ingramcontent.com/pod-product-compliance
Lightning Source LLC
Chambersburg PA
CBHW052106090426
42741CB00009B/1693